Name _____ Date _____

Chapter 2 Test: Egyptians Lived on the Nile River

A. Fill in the blanks.

1. The Nile River is on the continent of _____

2. Every year the Nile River would _____.

3. The people who lived in the Nile delta were called the _____.

4. The people who lived along the straight part of the Nile River were called the

   _____.

5. The king of Egypt became known as the _____.

B. Multiple Choice. Circle the letter of the best choice.

6. What is the Nile Delta?

    a. the area at the top of the river where it splits into several different little rivers

    b. the name of the mountain range near the Nile River

    c. the part of the river that dried up each year

7. Why did the Egyptian farmers like to see the river flood?

    a. It would give them more drinking water.

    b. It would make the air cooler.

    c. It would bring up rich dirt that was good for the plants.

    d. It would make it easier to fish.

8. How many tribes lived along the Nile during Egypt's early history?

    a. one

    b. two

    c. three

    d. four

9. When the Egyptians were united, what did the king wear to show that he ruled the entire country?

      a. a red crown

      b. a shepherd's crook

      c. a double crown with a white spike at the center and a red band on the outside

      d. a gold crown

10. According to one Egyptian myth, Set tricked his brother, Osiris, into lying down in a _____.

      a. river

      b. field

      c. bed

      d. coffin

11. What happened to Osiris after he lay down?

      a. Set threw him into the river.

      b. Ra helped him climb out.

      c. He was buried.

      d. He cried until he had no tears left.

12. What happened after Osiris came back to life?

      a. Isis wrapped him in linen so that he became the first mummy.

      b. The Nile filled back up and overflowed.

      c. Set built a beautiful coffin for him.

      d. The Nile wept over his death and ran dry.

C. True or False. Write the word "true" or "false."

_____ 13. When the White Crown King and the Red Crown King fought for control of Egypt, the White Crown King won.

_____ 14. The Egyptians worshipped many gods.

_____ 15. Osiris was the god of the sun and the chief god.

_____ 16. The Egyptian pharaoh was worshipped as a god.

_____ 17. Egyptian farmers would build their houses very close to the river.

_____ 18. Egyptian stories about the gods often tried to explain why the Nile overflowed each year.

The Story of the World

Chapter 3 Test: The First Writing

A. Fill in the blanks.

1 The _____ were among the earliest people to use writing.

2. They wrote with pictures called _____.

3. The people who lived in _____ found a better way to write using wet clay.

4. They wrote with pictures called _____.

B. Multiple Choice. Circle the letter of the best choice.

5. The Egyptians carved their pictures into _____.

    a. stone tablets

    b. wet clay

    c. sand

    d. paper

6. Where is Mesopotamia?

    a. in Egypt

    b. below the Nile River

    c. between the Tigris and Euphrates Rivers

    d. next to Egypt

7. What did the Sumerians do with their tablets after they carved them?

    a. get them wet to harden them

    b. bake them until they were hard

    c. roll them up into scrolls

    d. fold them up

8. The Egyptians learned to make a special kind of paper called _____.

    a. meso

    b. cuneiform

    c. hieroglyphics

    d. papyrus

9. What is something that is not good about this special paper?

    a. It starts to fall apart over time.

    b. It is easier to write on paper than on clay or stone.

    c. It can be folded or rolled up into a scroll.

    d. It takes up less room.

10. We do not know a great deal about what happened in Egypt after they started writing on _____ because these writings have crumbled and disappeared.

    a. stone

    b. wet clay

    c. paper

C. True or False. Write the word "true" or "false."

_____ 11. The stone tablets carved by the Egyptians lasted for a long time and they were quick to make.

_____ 12. Writing in clay was harder than carving in stone.

_____ 13. The word Mesopotamia means "between two rivers."

_____ 14. Egyptian paper was made from reeds that grew along the banks of the Nile.

_____ 15. We know a lot about early Egyptian and Sumerian history because of the writings that have been found.

Name _____ Date _____

Chapter 4 Test: The Old Kingdom of Egypt

A. Fill in the blanks.

1. During the Old Kingdom of Egypt, the Egyptians began to make _____ for the first time.

2. Only _____ were allowed to embalm bodies.

3. The Egyptians believed that the _____ would be weighed on a special pair of scales when a person reached the afterworld.

4. A mummy was put into _____ coffins before it was buried.

5. Pharaohs were buried in _____ to keep their treasures safe.

B. Multiple Choice. Circle the letter of the best choice.

6. How long did it take to make a mummy?

    a. several days

    b. over two months

    c. two weeks

    d. one year

7. What did the priests do with most of the organs inside a dead body?

    a. They were covered in special spices and placed in canopic jars.

    b. They were covered in special spices and placed back in the body.

    c. They were wrapped in linen strips.

    d. They were covered with gold.

8. What was placed between the strips of linen wrapped around a mummy?

    a. salt

    b. spices

    c. wine

    d. pieces of jewelry

9. A _____ was put onto the mummy's face so that the gods would recognize him.

    a. sarcophagus

    b. gold mask

    c. beautiful painting

    d. papyrus

10. What were the pyramids made out of?

    a. stone

    b. clay

    c. gold

    d. wood

11. How did the Egyptians build the pyramids?

    a. They used elephants to drag the blocks.

    b. They built ramps and used ropes.

    c. They used cranes and bulldozers.

    d. They carved the pyramids out of mountains.

C. True or False. Write the word "true" or "false."

_____ 12. The Egyptians believed it was important to embalm a body so that the dead could enter the afterworld.

_____ 13. The burial chamber would be filled with everything that a dead person would need in the afterlife such as furniture, food, clothes, games, and jewelry.

_____ 14. A sarcophagus was a big stone coffin inside the burial chamber.

_____ 15. Once a tomb was sealed it was never again opened or disturbed by robbers.

_____ 16. The Great Sphinx is an imaginary animal with the body of a man and the head of a lion.

The Story of the World

Chapter 5 Test: The First Sumerian Dictator

A. Fill in the blanks.

1. _____ is the area of land between the Tigris and Euphrates rivers.

2. The _____ lived in this area.

3. The cities in Sumer were called _____ because each city was like a separate country with its own king and army.

4. A man named _____ wanted to make all of the cities into one country.

5. He grew up in the city of _____.

B. Multiple Choice. Circle the letter of the best choice.

6. What did the villages in Sumer build to protect themselves?

    a. fences

    b. clay tablets

    c. castles

    d. thick walls with high towers

7. Sargon became the _____ in the king's palace.

    a. cook

    b. cup bearer

    c. soldier

    d. general

8. Sargon became so popular that he convinced the _____ to follow him.

    a. army

    b. king

    c. farmers

    d. queen

9. How did Sargon unite all of the cities in Mesopotamia?

    a. He poisoned all of the other kings.

    b. He became very popular with all of the people.

    c. He fought over fifty wars.

10. Sargon named his new empire _____.

    a. Sargonia

    b. Sumer

    c. Akkadia

    d. Mesopotamia

C. True or False. Write the word "true" or "false."

_____ 11. One story about Sargon says that he was found floating down the Euphrates River in a basket when he was a baby.

_____ 12. Sargon convinced the army to kill the king.

_____ 13. All of the cities in Mesopotamia were glad that Sargon was their new king.

_____ 14. Sargon sent police to every city to make sure the people were following his laws.

_____ 15. A military dictatorship is when a ruler uses his army to make sure people obey him.

The Story of the World

Chapter 6 Test: The Jewish People

A. Fill in the blanks.

1. Abram lived in one of the cities in Sargon's empire called _____.

2. The Bible tells the story of Abram in the book of _____.

3. God told Abram to move to the land of _____.

4. Abraham's grandson, Jacob, had _____ sons.

5. Jacob's son, Joseph, became a powerful leader in _____.

B. Multiple Choice. Circle the letter of the best choice.

6. Abram's father, Terah, was worried that _____.

    a. Babylon might attack Ur and he would lose all of his riches

    b. he did not have enough money

    c. the moon-god would not protect him

    d. Abraham did not have a son to carry on the family business

7. Terah moved his family, including Abram and Sarai, to _____.

    a. Babylon

    b. Egypt

    c. Haran

    d. Canaan

8. When Abraham was 100 years old, he had a son named _____.

    a. Benjamin

    b. Judah

    c. Jacob

    d. Isaac

9. What special gift did Jacob give to Joseph?

    a. a beautiful coat

    b. a flock of sheep

    c. his own servant

    d. a shepherd's crook

10. What did Joseph's brothers do to him?

    a. They killed him.

    b. They sold him to traders as a slave.

    c. They threw him in a pit and left him there.

    d. They made fun of him.

11. The Pharaoh of Egypt had a dream about _____.

    a. vines and grapes

    b. bread baskets and birds

    c. the sun, moon, and stars

    d. seven fat cows and seven skinny cows

12. What did Pharaoh do after Joseph told him what his dream meant?

    a. He killed Joseph.

    b. He sent Joseph back to Canaan.

    c. He made Joseph second in command in Egypt.

    d. He gave Joseph to Potiphar.

C. True or False. Write the word "true" or "false."

_____ 13. Abraham means "father of many children."

_____ 14. There were ten tribes that became known as the nation of Israel, or the Jewish people.

_____ 15. God promised to bless Abraham if Abraham would worship only God.

_____ 16. Joseph's brothers were jealous of the special gift that Jacob gave to Joseph.

_____ 17. When Joseph's brothers came to Egypt to buy food during the famine, they recognized Joseph immediately.

_____ 18. When the Israelites moved to Egypt, they began to worship the same gods that the Egyptians worshipped.

Name _____ Date _____

Chapter 7 Test: Hammurabi and the Babylonians

A. Fill in the blanks.

1. Hammurabi ruled the whole southern part of Mesopotamia called _____.

2. He wrote down a set of laws called _____.

3. The Babylonians called the time that it took the earth to go all the way around the sun once _____.

4. They divided this time period into _____ months.

B. Multiple Choice. Circle the letter of the best choice.

5. Hammurabi wanted his empire to be governed by _____.

    a. just laws

    b. a strong army

    c. religious priests

    d. a powerful king

6. Why are Hammurabi's laws important?

    a. They are all fair laws.

    b. These laws are still used today.

    c. God gave them to him.

    d. They are the first set of written laws that we know of.

7. Who had to obey these laws?

    a. only men

    b. everyone but the king

    c. everyone

    d. only soldiers

8. Where did Hammurabi write down his laws?

    a. They were written on a scroll in a ziggurat .

    b. They were written on clay tablets.

    c. They were carved on the walls of the palace.

    d. They were carved on a stone monument.

9. Hammurabi encouraged his people to learn more about _____.

    a. the gods

    b. the laws of other cities

    c. farming

    d. nature

10. People in Babylon believed that they could find out what the gods were doing by _____.

    a. praying and offering sacrifices

    b. watching the movements of the planets and stars

    c. asking the priests

    d. observing nature

C. True or False. Write the word "true" or "false."

_____ 11. The people of Mesopotamia lived with war all the time because the citystates were constantly fighting with each other.

_____ 12. Hammurabi believed that the chief god of Babylon, Marduk, made him king so that he could become rich.

_____ 13. Hammurabi wanted people to follow his laws because they were right—not because soldiers were making them obey.

_____ 14. The Babylonians could tell the difference between stars and planets.

_____ 15. The Babylonians divided an hour into 50 minutes.

The Story of the World

Chapter 8 Test: The Assyrians

A. Fill in the blanks.

1. Shamshi-Adad ruled the _____ part of Mesopotamia.

2. The name of his empire was the _____ Empire.

3. The story of _____ is one of the oldest fairy-tales in the world.

4. According to this story, a _____ ate a magic plant that made it live forever.

B. Multiple Choice. Circle the letter of the best choice.

5. Where did Shamshi-Adad live?

    a. Babylon

    b. Assur

    c. Kish

    d. Egypt

6. Shamshi-Adad wanted to _____.

    a. be a fair ruler

    b. rule the whole world

    c. become a priest

    d. be a noble king

7. How did Shamshi get people to obey him?

    a. He killed anyone who would not do exactly what he said.

    b. He rewarded the people who obeyed him.

    c. He had fair laws.

    d. He promised to let the people choose their own leaders.

8. What did the people in Mesopotamia think of the Assyrians?

    a. They thought the Assyrians were fair rulers.

    b. They did not think that the Assyrians were good warriors.

    c. They thought the Assyrians had good laws.

    d. They were scared of the Assyrians.

9. What happened after Shamshi-Adad died?

    a. His two sons ruled together peacefully.

    b. Gilgamesh became the new ruler.

    c. Hammurabi conquered the Assyrians.

    d. His two sons split his empire.

10. According the story of Gilgamesh, what did the sky god, Anu, send to help the people?

    a. a monster named Enkidu

    b. a new king

    c. a man named Utnapishtim

    d. a strong army

C. True or False. Write the word "true" or "false."

_____ 11. Shamshi-Adad ruled by fear and cruelty.

_____ 12. Hammurabi was not as cruel as Shamshi-Adad.

_____ 13. Gilgamesh was a good king, and his people loved him.

_____ 14. Gilgamesh and Enkidu eventually became good friends.

_____ 15. According to the story, Gilgamesh ate a magic plant that made him live forever.

The Story of the World

Chapter 9 Test: The First Cities of India

A. Fill in the blanks.

1   Ancient people began to make money by _____ with other cities.

2.   Many ancient cities were built near _____.

3.   The people of India built cities near the _____.

4.   Their cities were often built around huge circular mounds called _____.

B. Multiple Choice. Circle the letter of the best choice.

5.   Ancient cities often used rivers as a road because _____.

    a.   the people could not agree where to build roads

    b.   it was safer than building roads

    c.   it was easier and faster to travel by boat than across land

    d.   the people did not have enough money to build roads

6.   Farmers in India grew grain like the Mesopotamians, but they also grew _____.

    a.   corn and melons

    b.   rice and beans

    c.   cotton and melons

    d.   corn and rice

7.   Another way that the Indian farmer was different from the Mesopotamian farmer was he used _____.

    a.   elephants and water buffalo

    b.   boats to trade his crops

    c.   iron tools

    d.   canals to irrigate

8. Why were the cities in the Indus Valley built around citadels?

   a. to make it easier for the farmers to work together

   b. to protect the people in case enemies attacked

   c. to make transportation easier

   d. to help the people become rich

9. What were the houses in the Indus Valley made of?

   a. stone

   b. cedar logs

   c. animal skins

   d. mud bricks baked hard in ovens

10. One ancient story passed down in India tells of a hunter and a flock of _____.

   a. quail

   b. elephants

   c. water buffalo

   d. chickens

C. True or False. Write the word "true" or "false."

_____ 11. The people of India found that it was easier to travel over the mountains than to travel by sea.

_____ 12. The people of ancient India built comfortable houses with courtyards, wells, and even toilets and drains.

_____ 13. For hundreds of years, no one knew that the great cities of India ever existed because they had been deserted and covered with dirt and sand.

_____ 14. The cities of India were eventually united into one large kingdom.

_____ 15. No one knows for sure what happened to the citadel cities of India.

Name _____   Date _____

Chapter 10 Test: The Far East: Ancient China

A. Fill in the blanks.

1. The people of China first lived between the _____ River and the Yangtze River.

2. In China, the farmers grew a different kind of grain called _____.

3. The Empress Lei Zu discovered a way to make the fabric called _____.

4. A _____ is when a family rules one country for many years.

5. The Chinese used a special kind of writing called _____.

B. Multiple Choice. Circle the letter of the best choice.

6. Why was China called the "Far East"?

    a. The Chinese people had to travel far to the east to trade with other people.

    b. It was all the way the way to the edge of the world to the Mesopotamians.

    c. It was far away from the Yangtze River.

    d. The Yangtze River was east of China.

7. How did Lei Zu discover the new kind of fabric?

    a. She had a dream about it.

    b. Her servant girl told her how to make it.

    c. A cocoon fell into her cup of tea.

    d. She saw some cocoons in a tree and thought they would make pretty fabric.

8. Why don't we know many facts about the first great leader of China?

    a. Many of the written records say different things.

    b. There are no written records about his empire.

    c. There are no stories or legends about him.

    d. No one understands Chinese writing.

9.   During the rule of the Shang family, the Chinese began to use _____.

     a. bronze

     b. gold

     c. silver

     d. iron

10. The Shang family also used a kind of writing in which words look like _____.

     a. straight lines

     b. wavy lines

     c. letters

     d. pictures

11. What kind of animals did farmers in China raise?

     a. sheep and goats

     b. elephants and water buffalo

     c. turkeys and geese

     d. pigs, chickens, and cows

12. What kind of soil did the Chinese farmers need to raise their special kind of grain?

     a. very wet soil

     b. very dry soil

     c. soil that is wet part of the year and dry part of the year

     d. rocky soil

C. True or False. Write the word "true" or "false."

_____ 13. Huang Di was the first great leader of China who united the many small villages into one empire.

_____ 14. The Shang dynasty ruled for about 500 years.

_____ 15. The mulberry plant was an important plant in Ancient China.

_____ 16. In the story about Chin, it was the mother's duty to make sure that the father had everything that he needed in the morning.

_____ 17. Chin's job helping his father in the fields was very easy.

_____ 18. The rivers in China often flooded.

The Story of the World

Chapter 11 Test: Ancient Africa

A. Fill in the blanks.

1. The _____ is a large, dry, and hot area west of Egypt.

2. The only water in this area is found in an _____, a little patch of land where water collects and a few scrubby palm trees can grow.

3. This area in Africa was not always dry; it was once a green, fertile place full of trees and _____.

4. _____ is a favorite character of African storytellers.

B. Multiple Choice. Circle the letter of the best choice.

5. Why don't we know much about ancient Africa?

    a. The people of Africa didn't leave written records or thousands of artifacts.

    b. Many of the written records say different things.

    c. We have no stories or legends from Africa.

    d. No one understands African writing.

6. What did archeologists find when they dug down through the hard dirt of the Sahara?

    a. clay tablets with writing on them

    b. bronze weapons

    c. thousands and thousands of artifacts

    d. pollen from trees and seeds from grasses and flowers that do not grow in the Sahara today

7. What happened in the Sahara?

    a. The rains got scarcer and the grass and trees dried up.

    b. Too much rain flooded it.

    c. Many of the tribes of people who lived there fought wars and killed each other.

    d. The Egyptians conquered the tribes of people.

8. Where did the people who once lived in the Sahara move?

    a. east to Egypt

    b. south to the center of Africa

    c. east to Mesopotamia

    d. north to the coast of the Mediterranean Sea

9. Which word best describes Anansi?

    a. honest

    b. tricky

    c. brave

    d. fearful

10. What kinds of food did Anansi find in the different villages?

    a. yams and rice

    b. wheat and corn

    c. rice and melons

    d. cassava, plantains, and rice

C. True or False. Write the word "true" or "false."

_____ 11. The people who once lived in the Sahara were farmers, just like those who lived in the Fertile Crescent.

_____ 12. Archeologists have found paintings on the walls of caves that show how Africans once lived.

_____ 13. Yams are like sweet potatoes.

_____ 14. Plantains are a special kind of rice.

_____ 15. The people of Africa passed many stories down from person to person.

The Story of the World

Chapter 12 Test: The Middle Kingdom of Egypt

A. Fill in the blanks.

1. When Amenemhet became pharaoh, he wanted to make Egypt larger, so he decided to conquer the country to the south of Egypt called _____.

2. The Egyptians renamed this country _____.

3. Amenemhet's family ruled Egypt for many years and became a powerful _____.

4. Nomads from _____ called the Hyksos conquered Egypt after Amenemhet's family ruled.

B. Multiple Choice. Circle the letter of the best choice.

5. What happened to the Old Kingdom of Egypt?

    a. It grew much larger when the people conquered the land of Canaan.

    b. It grew more powerful.

    c. It became weak and powerless.

    d. It was conquered by the Nubians.

6. Amenemhet's reign was the beginning of the _____.

    a. The Middle Kingdom of Egypt

    b. The Old Kingdom of Egypt

    c. The New Kingdom of Egypt

    d. The Second Kingdom of Egypt

7. Amenemhet knew there was _____ in the hills and ground of the country to the south of Egypt.

    a. bronze

    b. silver

    c. ivory

    d. gold

8. When the people to the south of Egypt were conquered by the Egyptians, they _____.

    a. became Egyptian

    b. moved to Canaan

    c. rebelled against the Egyptians

    d. moved to the Sahara

9. After Amenemhet's family ruled, Egypt once again became _____.

    a. stronger and more powerful

    b. weak and powerless

    c. larger

    d. richer

10. The Egyptians thought that the Hyksos were _____.

    a. good rulers

    b. rude, unclean, and uncivilized

    c. prosperous and wealthy

    d. polite and good-looking

11. Who drove the Hyksos out of Egypt?

    a. Amenemhet

    b. the Egyptian priests

    c. a group of Egyptian princes

    d. the Canaanites

C. True or False. Write the word "true" or "false."

_____ 12. Egypt became stronger even when there were bad pharaohs.

_____ 13. One woman from the conquered country to the south became the queen of Egypt.

_____ 14. The Hyksos used the same kind of weapons that the Egyptians used.

_____ 15. The Hyksos called the Egyptians "shepherd kings."

_____ 16. Using the weapons of the Hyksos, the Egyptians became one of the most powerful kingdoms in the whole world

Name _____ Date _____

Chapter 13 Test: The New Kingdom of Egypt

A. Matching. Match each pharaoh with the correct description.

_____ 1. Hatshepsut   a. fought both the Nubians and the Hyksos and made Egypt twice as big

       2. Amenhotep   b. became pharaoh even though she was a woman; wore men's clothes and a false beard

_____ 3. Thutmose   c. was only seven when he became king; was buried with many treasures that were not found until three thousand years later

_____ 4. Tutankhamen   d. wanted the Egyptians to worship just one god

B. True or False. Write the word "true" or "false."

_____ 5. Before he became pharaoh, Thutmose was a general in the Egyptian army.

_____ 6. Most Egyptians worshipped only one god.

_____ 7. Polytheism is the worship of just one god.

_____ 8. When Tut's tomb was discovered, many items had already been stolen.

_____ 9. After it was discovered, people said that there was a curse on Tut's tomb.

C. Multiple Choice. Circle the letter of the best choice.

10. The New Kingdom of Egypt is sometimes called the _____.

   a. Middle Kingdom of Egypt

   b. Second Kingdom of Egypt

   c. Last Kingdom of Egypt

   d. Golden Age of Egypt

11. How did Thutmose become the pharaoh of Egypt?

   a. He married the pharaoh's daughter.

   b. He killed the old pharaoh.

   c. He persuaded the army to crown him as king.

   d. The priests named him as the new pharaoh.

12. Thutmose did not try to conquer Babylon because _____.

    a. He knew Babylon was too powerful to conquer.

    b. Babylon was too far away.

    c. His army did not want to cross the Euphrates River.

    d. He thought that Babylon did not have enough gold or riches.

13. Which of the following were Egyptian women not allowed to do?

    a. get married and have children

    b. serve at the temple

    c. rule as pharaoh

    d. become dancers

14. As pharaoh, Hatshepsut _____.

    a. fought many wars

    b. brought back gold, incense, monkeys, and elephants from Africa

    c. worshipped only one god

    d. ruled for only four years

15. A monotheist is someone who _____.

    a. worships many gods

    b. worships only one god

    c. worships no gods

    d. does not believe in any gods

16. When Amenhotep died, the Egyptian people _____.

    a. buried him with all of his treasures

    b. built many monuments to him

    c. worshipped only one god

    d. tried to forget he had ever been pharaoh

17. The Valley of the Kings is a place in Egypt where _____.

    a. many of the pharaohs lived

    b. the pyramids are located

    c. many of the pharaohs were buried

    d. archeologists have found old temples

Name _____ Date _____

The Story of the World

Chapter 14 Test: The Israelites Leave Egypt

A. Fill in the blanks.

1. The Israelites are descended from _____.

2. The Egyptians made the Israelites their _____.

3. _____ was an Israelite who grew up in the palace of the pharaoh.

4. When the Israelites left Egypt, God parted the waters of the _____.

5. The story of the Israelites leaving Egypt is found in the Bible in the book of _____.

B. Multiple Choice. Circle the letter of the best choice.

6. The Israelites were unusual in the ancient world because _____.

    a. they were monotheists

    b. they were polytheists

    c. they were very rich

    d. they had very small families

7. Why did the Israelites move to Egypt?

    a. They were trying to escape from the Babylonians.

    b. They wanted to conquer the Egyptians.

    c. They were looking for gold.

    d. There was a famine in Canaan where they lived.

8. The Egyptians started to worry that the Israelites might _____.

    a. try to steal all of their gold

    b. decide to move back to Canaan

    c. attack the Egyptians and take their kingdom away

    d. start worshipping the Egyptian gods

9. What did the pharaoh decide to do about the Israelites?

    a. make the Israelites worship the Egyptian gods

    b. send the Israelites back to Canaan

    c. kill every Israelite baby boy

    d. send the Israelites to the Sahara Desert

10 Who found a baby floating in a basket on the Nile?

    a. pharaoh's daughter

    b. pharaoh

    c. Miriam

    d. a servant girl

11. God sent _____ plagues on Egypt to show that he was more powerful than the gods of Egypt.

    a. five

    b. ten

    c. eight

    d. six

12. Where did the Israelites go when they left Egypt?

    a. to the coast of the Mediterranean Sea

    b. to the Sahara Desert

    c. to Mesopotamia

    d. back toward Canaan

C. True or False. Write the word "true" or "false."

_____ 13. While they lived in Egypt, the Israelites worshipped only one God.

_____ 14. The Israelite nation grew smaller and smaller in Egypt.

_____ 15. Moses was born into an Egyptian family and was raised in the palace.

_____ 16. When the Israelites asked to leave Egypt, pharaoh said yes.

_____ 17. When the Israelites left Egypt, the Egyptians chased them, but were drowned.

_____ 18. The Israelites later became a powerful kingdom in their own right.

The Story of the World

Chapter 15 Test: The Phoenicians

A. Fill in the blanks.

1. The Phoenicians were the group of people living in _____.

2. The Phoenicians sailed all around the _____.

3. Two important Phoenician cities were _____ and

4. _____.

B. Multiple Choice. Circle the letter of the best choice.

5. Which of these sentences is not true about the area where the Phoenicians lived?

    a. It was rocky, sandy, and dry.

    b. It wasn't a good place to raise animals because there wasn't enough grass or water.

    c. It was surrounded by steep craggy hills.

    d. It was easy to get into and out of.

6. What did the Phoenicians use to make glass?

    a. snails

    b. sand and lye

    c. rocks

    d. cedar logs

7. What was the color of the Phoenicians' famous dye?

    a. green

    b. blue

    c. purple

    d. gold

8. The Phoenicians used _____ to make their special dye.

    a. flowers

    b. lye

    c. snails

    d. cedar logs

9. The color of this dye was often called "the color of kings" because _____.

     a. the dye was so expensive

     b. only kings were allowed to wear it

     c. it was the Phoenician king's favorite color

     d. the dye smelled so good when it was being made

10. The Phoenicians started _____, little settlements of people, in many of the places where their ships landed.

     a. states

     b. city-states

     c. colonies

     d. countries

C. True or False. Write the word "true" or "false."

_____ 11. When the Israelites walked from Egypt back up to Canaan, they were moving into an empty country.

_____ 12. The northern part of Canaan wasn't a very good place to grow wheat.

_____ 13. The Phoenicians were the first glassmakers to invent glass blowing.

_____ 14. According to the story, Dido left her home because she was afraid of her husband.

_____ 15. Dido wanted to build her city near the water so that ships would visit and trade with her.

The Story of the World

Chapter 16 Test: The Return of Assyria

A. Fill in the blanks.

1. The Assyrian army used shields made out of _____.

2. Ashurbanipal was a _____ king.

3. He lived in the city of _____.

4. He was the first _____.

B. Multiple Choice. Circle the letter of the best choice.

5. Which of these countries did the Assyrians not conquer?

   a. Babylon

   b. Egypt

   c. India

   d. Canaan

6. What did Ashurbanipal like to do for fun?

   a. write poetry

   b. hunt lions with bows and arrows

   c. make glass

   d. listen to music

7. The Assyrians were almost impossible to beat because they _____.

   a. fought in pairs

   b. used bronze swords

   c. dug tunnels under the ground

   d. wore so much armor

8. What did most of the people in the Assyrian Empire think about Ashurbanipal?

   a. They hated him.

   b. They thought he was a fair ruler.

   c. They admired him.

   d. They were happy to obey him.

9. What did Ashurbanipal do so that people would remember him?

    a. He held a grand parade.

    b. He told many stories.

    c. He built a beautiful temple.

    d. He collected many books.

10. During Ashurbanipal's time, books were made out of _____.

    a. paper

    b. stone

    c. clay

    d. scrolls

C. True or False. Write the word "true" or "false."

_____ 11. To defeat the Babylonians, the Assyrians dug canals and flooded the city.

_____ 12. The Assyrians conquered the Israelites and never allowed them to return to Canaan.

_____ 13. To capture a city, Assyrian soldiers would dig tunnels under the city walls.

_____ 14. Ashurbanipal built beautiful gardens with strange plants from far away.

_____ 15. Ashurbanipal created the first hospital in the world.

The Story of the World

Chapter 17 Test: Babylon Takes Over Again!

A. Fill in the blanks.

1. Babylon had a powerful king who went mad and lived like a wild _____.

2. This story is recorded in the Bible in the book of _____.

3. The king of Babylon was worried about _____, a country to the east.

4. This king also built the _____ of Babylon for his wife. They are one of the Seven Wonders of the Ancient World.

B. Multiple Choice. Circle the letter of the best choice.

5. What was the name of the great king of Babylon?

   a. Nebuchadnezzar

   b. Ashurbanipal

   c. Marduk

   d. Ishtar

6. Which country was never conquered by the Babylonians?

   a. Assyria

   b. Canaan

   c. Egypt

7. What did the Babylonians do to the city of Nineveh?

   a. They made it their new capital.

   b. They destroyed it.

   c. They left it alone.

   d. They flooded it.

8. The king of Babylon built a famous _____ to honor the chief goddess, Ishtar.

   a. gate

   b. garden

   c. library

   d. temple

9. The king of Babylon went mad because _____.

    a. his wife was so sad

    b. he was weary from fighting so many wars

    c. he was so worried about other nations attacking him

    d. he thought he was greater than everyone, including God

10. Who did the king of Babylon marry?

    a. the queen of Egypt

    b. the princess of the country to the east

    c. an Israelite princess

    d. a princess from Assyria

11. What did she miss the most about her old home?

    a. her palace

    b. the flat land

    c. the mountains

    d. her family

C. True or False. Write the word "true" or "false."

_____ 12. The Babylonians forgave the Assyrians for destroying Babylon.

_____ 13. The Babylonian Empire was not as large as the Assyrian Empire.

_____ 14. After the king of Babylon lost his mind, he never got better.

_____ 15. The king of Babylon married his wife because he thought she was the most beautiful woman he had ever seen.

_____ 16. The new queen of Babylon was homesick.

The Story of the World

Chapter 18 Test: Life in Early Crete

A. Fill in the blanks.

1. The _____ lived on an island called Crete.

2. Crete is a long, skinny island in the _____ Sea.

3. The people of Crete used to entertain themselves by leaping over _____.

4. The people of Crete had the first _____, an army that fights on water.

5. The _____ was a monster who was half man and half bull.

B. Multiple Choice. Circle the letter of the best choice.

6. The people of Crete held their leaping festivals to honor _____.

    a. the king

    b. their gods

    c. their children

    d. nature

7. Why was it so dangerous to travel on the sea in ancient times?

    a. The weather made the water rough and choppy.

    b. There were no maps so the people did not know where to sail.

    c. Pirates controlled the sea.

    d. The people did not know how to make boats.

8. King _____ was a legendary king of Crete.

    a. Nebuchadnezzar

    b. Minos

    c. Aegeus

    d. Ariadne

9. This king fed _____ to the monster that lived in the maze beneath his palace.

    a. girls and boys from a nearby city

    b. his slaves

    c. bulls

    d. his daughters

10. Theseus was the prince of the nearby city, _____.

    a. Egypt

    b. Nineveh

    c. Knossos

    d. Athens

11. What did Theseus use to find his way through the maze so he could kill the monster?

    a. a map

    b. a mirror

    c. a ball of wool

    d. a sword

12. When Theseus was sailing home, his father _____.

    a. jumped off a cliff

    b. ran to the shore to meet him

    c. planned a huge celebration to welcome him home

    d. was killed by one of his enemies

13. Many historians believe the people left Crete because _____.

    a. a hurricane forced them to leave

    b. they were tired of living on an island

    c. a volcano erupted nearby

    d. pirates captured them

C. True or False. Write the word "true" or "false."

_____ 14. The children who participated in the leaping festivals had a safe job.

_____ 15. These children were given beautiful clothes, jewelry, and gold.

_____ 16. Ariadne helped Theseus kill the monster.

_____ 17. The Aegean Sea was named after the father of Ariadne.

_____ 18. The island of Thera sank into the sea.

The Story of the World

Chapter 19 Test: The Early Greeks

A. Matching. Match each group of people with the correct description.

_____ 1. Mycenaeans   a. also called the Sea people; they conquered the Greeks

_____ 2. Dorians   b. invaded Greece from the North

_____ 3. Philistines   c. Greek people who conquered the island of Crete

_____ 4. Minoans   d. lived on the island of Crete

B. Multiple Choice. Circle the letter of the best choice.

5. The Mycenaeans built _____ all around the Aegean Sea.

    a. colonies

    b. palaces

    c. walls

    d. temples

6. The Mycenaeans were good fighters because they made their weapons and armor from _____.

    a. bronze

    b. wood

    c. gold

    d. iron

7. The Mycenaeans were the first Greeks to use _____ in battle.

    a. javelins

    b. swords

    c. horses

    d. bows and arrows

8. How did the Mycenaeans live?

    a. The wandered around from place to place.

    b. They lived in houses made of stone or wood.

    c. They lived in caves.

d. The built tents with sticks and animal hides.

9. How were the barbarians different from the Mycenaeans?

    a. The barbarians had regular jobs.

    b. The barbarians lived in better houses.

    c. The barbarians couldn't read or write.

    d. The barbarians were great craftsmen.

10. The barbarians had _____ weapons.

    a. wooden

    b. gold

    c. bronze

    d. iron

11. The barbarians used _____ to kill Greek chariot drivers from a long distance away.

    a. swords

    b. javelins

    c. horses

    d. cannons

12. The time period after the Greeks were conquered is called the _____.

    a. Dark Ages

    b. Golden Age

    c. Mycenaean Era

    d. Missing Time Era

C. True or False. Write the word "true" or "false."

_____ 13. The Mycenaeans learned how to build ships from the Minoans.

_____ 14. The Mycenaeans were the first great Greek civilization.

_____ 15. The barbarians thought the Greeks were ignorant, smelly and uncivilized.

_____ 16. We know much about the barbarians who conquered the Greeks because they left many written records.

Name _____   Date _____

Chapter 20 Test: Greece Gets Civilized Again

A. Matching. Match each person with the correct description.

_____ 1. Poseidon   a. a Greek poet who wrote down some of the old Greek stories

2. Cyclops   b. a Greek warrior who fought in the Trojan War

_____ 3. Homer   c. a giant with only one eye in the center of his forehead

_____ 4. Odysseus   d. the Greek god of the sea

B. Multiple Choice. Circle the letter of the best choice.

5. What happened to the barbarians who invaded Greece?

   a. They moved back to their original lands.

   b. They were eventually defeated by the Mycenaeans.

   c. They became civilized and learned to live like the Greeks.

   d. The were killed when a volcano erupted.

6. What kind of crops did the Greeks learn to grow?

   a. olives, grapes, and figs

   b. corn and beans

   c. oranges and cotton

   d. yams and bananas

7. For fun, the Greeks liked to _____.

   a. dance

   b. attack their neighbors

   c. sing

   d. draw pictures

8. We know more about the early Greeks than we know about the barbarians because they wrote things down using their own _____.

   a. pens

   b. alphabet

   c. pictograms

   d. cuneiforms

9. According to tradition, what was wrong with Homer?

    a. He did not know how to write.

    b. He was deaf.

    c. He could not walk.

    d. He was blind.

10. One famous Greek story tells about a war when the Greeks attacked the city of _____.

    a. Knossos

    b. Troy

    c. Mycenae

    d. Nineveh

11. The Greeks held _____ to honor Zeus and to celebrate courage and strength.

    a. the Olympic Games

    b. the Trojan Games

    c. chariot races

    d. yearly wars

12. The pentathlon was an athletic event in which the athlete had to compete in _____ different events.

    a. ten

    b. four

    c. five

    d. seven

C. True or False. Write the word "true" or "false."

_____ 13. Many of the letters we use today are borrowed from the ancient Greeks.

_____ 14. The Phoenicians had one of the first alphabets.

_____ 15. The *Iliad* is a poem about a Greek soldier trying to sail back home.

_____ 16. To escape from the giant's cave, the Greek soldiers held on to the bellies of the giant's sheep.

_____ 17. Both men and women were allowed to compete in the Olympic Games.

_____ 18. The Olympic Games were held every six years.

The Story of the World

Chapter 21 Test: The Medes and the Persians

A. Fill in the blanks.

1. The Babylonians and the _____ finally defeated the Assyrians.

2. The Persians were a tribe of _____ who lived at the edge of Media.

3. _____ became a great king of Persia.

4. This king became the greatest king in the world at that time, but there was still one country that he had not conquered. This country was _____.

B. Multiple Choice. Circle the letter of the best choice.

5. What did King Astyges of Persia do with his grandson?

   a. He ordered his chief advisor to kill him.

   b. He gave him many gifts of gold and jewels.

   c. He taught him how to be a great king.

   d. He trained him to be a shepherd.

6. Harpagus disobeyed his master by _____.

   a. not worshipping the king's gods

   b. letting the king's grandson run away

   c. not punishing the Persians when they did not follow the king's laws

   d. ordering a shepherd to kill the baby instead of doing it himself

7. _____ helped Cyrus become king.

   a. Astyges

   b. Croesus

   c. Harpagus

   d. Shamshi-Adad

8. The Persians thought Cyrus was a great warrior and a _____ king.

   a. selfish

   b. lazy

   c. cruel

   d. good and fair

9. Croesus had more _____ than anyone in the world.

    a. gold

    b. land

    c. palaces

    d. soldiers

10. Cyrus was able to easily conquer Babylon because _____.

    a. the Babylonian Empire was not very strong.

    b. the city did not have a wall around it.

    c. the Babylonians hated their king.

    d. he had many more soldiers than the Babylonian king.

11. When Cyrus became king of Babylon, he allowed the Jews to _____.

    a. have important positions in his government

    b. return to Palestine

    c. build their own temple in Persia

    d. elect their own king

12. The Jews called Cyrus _____.

    a. a cruel tyrant

    b. the Anointed of the Lord

    c. the King with the Golden Touch

    d. the shepherd king

C. True or False. Write the word "true" or "false."

_____ 13. The Assyrians and the Babylonians fought each other for many years, and the rulers of the world kept changing.

_____ 14. The Medes and the Babylonians also fought against each other.

_____ 15. Astyges was worried by a dream he had.

_____ 16. Cyrus was raised as a shepherd on a mountain.

_____ 17. When Cyrus grew up, he was smaller than all the other boys his age.

_____ 18. Cyrus conquered land from Egypt all the way to India.

The Story of the World

Chapter 22 Test: Sparta and Athens

A. Fill in the blanks.

1. The people of _____ wanted their children to be wise and educated.

2. The people of _____ wanted their children to be strong and brave.

3. When the citizens of Athens needed to vote about something, they would gather at a special meeting place called the _____.

4. A _____ is when people vote on the laws and the leaders.

B. Multiple Choice. Circle the letter of the best choice.

5. The Greeks were different from the Persians because all of the Greeks _____.

    a. didn't speak the same language

    b. didn't obey the same king

    c. didn't dress the same

    d. didn't worship the same gods

6. Sparta was ruled by _____ kings.

    a. many

    b. elected

    c. warrior

    d. educated

7. Spartan boys were never allowed to _____.

    a. complain

    b. run

    c. eat

    d. exercise

8. When Spartan boys were 20 years old, they had to _____.

    a. get married

    b. leave the army

    c. vote

    d. pass a test of fitness and bravery

9. What were girls in Sparta supposed to do?

   a. have children who would fight for Sparta

   b. learn to read and write

   c. join the army with the men

   d. learn to take care of the household

10. Which of these things did the people of Athens not vote on?

    a. their leaders

    b. the gods they would worship

    c. their taxes

    d. whether they should go to war

11. The Athenians thought it was important to be educated so that _____.

    a. people could read

    b. citizens could understand how to vote properly

    c. people would have better jobs

    d. boys would know how to fight

12. _____ was a famous Greek who said ignorant people will always obey tyrants.

    a. Cyrus

    b. Sparta

    c. Athens

    d. Plato

13. What were all girls in Athens supposed to do?

    a. have children who would fight for Athens

    b. learn to read and write

    c. learn how to vote

    d. learn to take care of the household

C. True or False. Write the word "true" or "false."

_____ 14. Sparta and Athens were very similar cities.

_____ 15. All men in Sparta were allowed to vote.

_____ 16. Boys in Athens learned reading, writing, mathematics, music, and poetry.

_____ 17. Girls in Athens learned how to sew, raise a garden, and take care of children.

_____ 18. The people of Athens wanted to be ruled by tyrants.

The Story of the World

Chapter 23 Test: The Greek Gods

A. Matching. Match each person with the correct description.

_____ 1. Zeus   a   the king of the Greeks

_____ 2. Hera   b. the king of the gods

_____ 3. Aphrodite   c. the wife of Menelaus

_____ 4. Athena   d. the prince of Troy

_____ 5. Paris   e. the goddess of love and beauty

_____ 6. Helen   f. the wife of Zeus

_____ 7. Menelaus   g. the goddess of strife

_____ 8. Eris   h. the goddess of war

B. Multiple Choice. Circle the letter of the best choice.

9.   The Greeks were _____, which means they worshipped many gods.

   a. polyglots

   b. Confucians

   c. polytheists

   d. monotheists

10. The Greeks believed that their gods lived on _____, the highest mountain in Greece.

   a. Mount Olympus

   b. Mount Zion

   c. Mount Ararat

   d. Mount Sinai

11. Why did Zeus want to start a war on earth?

   a. He was bored.

   b. The goddess of war needed something to do.

   c. He liked having wars.

   d. He thought there were too many people on the earth.

12. What did Zeus make that caused a war?

    a. a golden crown

    b. a golden orange

    c. a crown of olive leaves

    d. a golden apple

13 _____ was asked to judge who was the most beautiful.

    a. Poseidon

    b. Paris

    c. Menelaus

    d. Eris

14. Why did he choose Aphrodite as the most beautiful?

    a. He wanted to be king of the whole world.

    b. He wanted to win every battle he fought.

    c. He wanted to have the most beautiful woman on earth.

    d. He wanted to obey Zeus.

15. What happened when Helen fell in love with Paris?

    a. The Trojan War began.

    b. Paris killed Menelaus.

    c. Hera killed Helen.

    d. Helen and Paris got married.

C. True or False. Write the word "true" or "false."

_____ 16. The Greeks believed that the gods were very interested in what men were doing.

_____ 17. The Greek gods were always kind and helpful to men.

_____ 18. The Trojan War lasted for many years.

The Story of the World

Chapter 24 Test: The Wars of the Greeks

A. Fill in the blanks.

1. Sparta and _____ were always fighting with each other.

2. These two cities decided to become friends and allies when _____ tried to invade Greece.

3. The _____ was a temple built in honor of Athena, the goddess of war.

4. _____ won the Peloponnesian War.

B. Multiple Choice. Circle the letter of the best choice.

5. The war with Persia lasted for _____.

    a. twenty years

    b. six weeks

    c. two months

    d. twenty-five years

6. Who was outnumbered at the Battle of Marathon?

    a. Sparta

    b. Salamis

    c. Persia

    d. Athens

7. After the Battle of Marathon, a messenger ran all the way to _____ to deliver the news of victory.

    a. Sparta

    b. Salamis

    c. Athens

    d. Persia

8. According to legend, what happened to the messenger?

    a. He became a hero.

    b. He died of exhaustion.

    c. He was made the new king.

9. When Greece was at peace they became famous for their _____.

    a. architecture

    b. food

    c. paintings

    d. books

10. What caused the Peloponnesian War?

    a. Sparta and Athens were afraid that another country would try to invade them again.

    b. The Greeks could not agree on the best kind of government.

    c. Sparta and Athens were afraid that the other city would become too powerful.

    d. Each Greek city wanted to have the most beautiful buildings and statues.

11. What happened in the city of Athens while Sparta was attacking them?

    a. The Persians joined with the Spartans.

    b. A plague broke out inside the city walls.

    c. The people began to starve to death.

    d. They ran out of water.

12. What did Alcibiades do that helped end the war?

    a. He convinced the Athenians to surrender.

    b. He became a traitor and led the Spartans into his own city.

    c. He killed the Spartan king.

    d. He killed the greatest Athenian general.

C. True or False. Write the word "true" or "false."

_____ 13. When the Persian king sent a messenger to Greece, the Greeks threw the messenger down a well.

_____ 14. During one battle, the Athenians refused to come help the Spartans because they were having a religious festival.

_____ 15. After the Battle of Marathon, Persia finally stopped attacking Greece.

_____ 16. A frieze is a picture carved in marble.

_____ 17. The people in Greek friezes look very real.

_____ 18. The Peloponnesian War lasted for sixty years.

Name _____ Date _____

Chapter 25 Test: Alexander the Great

A. Fill in the blanks.

1. Philip was the king of _____.

2. King Philip wanted to take over the _____ Empire, but he died before he could attack.

3. The Pharos was a giant _____.

4. Alexander built a great city named _____ in Egypt.

B. Multiple Choice. Circle the letter of the best choice.

5. The name "Alexander" means "ruler of _____."

   a. the world

   b. the sky

   c. men

   d. all people

6. Bucephalus was the name of Alexander's _____.

   a. father

   b. mother

   c. horse

   d. dog

7. What did Alexander do to the Gordian Knot?

   a. He cut it in half.

   b. He untied it.

   c. He burned it.

   d. He asked the gods to help him solve it.

8. Why was Alexander unable to conquer all of India?

    a. He did not know how to use elephants in battle.

    b. The Indian soldiers far outnumbered Alexander's soldiers.

    c. He died before he got to India.

    d. His soldiers refused to fight.

9. What did Alexander do so that people of the future would remember him?

    a. He built a huge library.

    b. He built many cities.

    c. He wrote many books.

    d. He had many statues made of himself.

10. How did Alexander die?

    a. His soldiers killed him.

    b. He caught the plague.

    c. He died of old age.

    d. No one knows for sure; he just became weaker and weaker.

11. After Alexander died, his generals divided his empire into _____ parts.

    a. two

    b. five

    c. three

    d. four

C. True or False. Write the word "true" or "false."

_____ 12. Egypt was the first area conquered by King Philip.

_____ 13. Alexander tamed his horse by turning him so he couldn't see his shadow.

_____ 14. Alexander was only 20 years old when he became king.

_____ 15. Ptolemy I became the new pharaoh of Egypt after the death of Alexander.

_____ 16. After Alexander died, his generals got along well together.

Name _____ Date _____

Chapter 26 Test: The People of the Americas

A. Fill in the blanks.

1. To get to the Americas from the Fertile Crescent, you have to cross the _____ Ocean.

2. The narrow strip of land that connects North and South America is called _____.

3. South America has flat, fertile land in the middle and _____ all along one edge.

4. The people of the Americas did not leave _____ behind so we don't know as much about them as we know about other ancient people.

B. Multiple Choice. Circle the letter of the best choice.

5. The _____ were a tribe of people who lived along the rivers of South America in a place that is now called Peru.

    a. Nazca

    b. Meso

    c. Olmecs

    d. Macedonians

6. These people made drawings on the ground that were _____.

    a. washed away by heavy rains

    b. carved in stone

    c. very small and hard to see

    d. hundreds of feet across

7. Some of these drawings were pictures of _____.

    a. their great tribal leaders

    b. horses, cows, and pigs

    c. spiders, hummingbirds, and flowers

    d. huge buildings and temples

8. Archeologists think these drawings may have been made using _____.

    a. roads and highways

    b. airplanes

    c. the sun

    d. mathematics

9. What was the name of the first civilization in Central America?

    a. Nazca

    b. Meso

    c. Olmecs

    d. Macedonians

10. Where did the rich people of this tribe live?

    a. on top of a huge pyramid of dirt and clay

    b. at the foot of the hill, on the plain

    c. in a city on a hill

    d. by the river

11. Archaeologists found huge _____ that once surrounded these people's temple.

    a. animals

    b. heads

    c. bodies

    d. pyramids

12. The people who lived in North America left us _____ that tell us about them.

    a. written records

    b. stories

    c. artifacts

    d. books

C. True or False. Write the word "true" or "false."

_____ 13. The ancient people of South America learned how to dry cassava roots, grind them up, and make them into banana pudding.

_____ 14. Mesoamerica means "between the Americas."

_____ 15. In the northern part of North America, the people ate corn, wheat, fish and buffalo.

_____ 16. The ancient people of North America were nomads.

The Story of the World

Chapter 27 Test: The Rise of Rome

A. Fill in the blanks.

1. Rome was founded on top of _____ hills.

2. Rome is located in the country of _____.

3. The most important Italian tribe was called the _____.

4. Their kings wore special robes called _____, with purple borders to show everyone how important the king was.

B. Multiple Choice. Circle the letter of the best choice.

5. According to the legend, who were Romulus and Remus?

   a. the first two Etruscan kings

   b. two brothers who founded Rome

   c. the first two consuls of Rome

   d. two of the Roman gods

6. Romulus and Remus were raised by _____.

   a. a wolf and then a shepherd

   b. their grandfather

   c. the servant who was told to drown them

   d. the king of Rome

7. Why did Romulus kill Remus?

   a. He was angry because Remus wanted to be king.

   b. He was jealous of Remus because their grandfather liked him better.

   c. He was angry because Remus jumped over his wall.

   d. He was tired of sharing everything with him.

8. The Etruscans traded with the _____.

   a. Phoenicians

   b. Egyptians

   c. Romans

   d. Greeks

9. Which of the following did the Romans not learn from the Etruscans?

    a. how to dress

    b. painting and music

    c. about the Greek gods

    d. how to fight

10. A _____ is a symbol of power that shows a bundle of rods with an ax blade.

    a. fasces

    b. consul

    c. dime

    d. patrician

11. Who could vote on laws and leaders in Rome?

    a. all men who weren't slaves

    b. only the rich and powerful men

    c. all of the men

    d. only the consuls

12. How many consuls were appointed in Rome?

    a. one

    b. ten

    c. five

    d. two

C. True or False. Write the word "true" or "false."

_____ 13. The Roman Empire lasted for hundreds and hundreds of years.

_____ 14. The Roman Empire was not as large as Alexander the Great's empire.

_____ 15. Ancient people liked stories about their kings that made them seem like great fairy-tale heroes.

_____ 16. Rome was a democracy just like Greece.

The Story of the World

Chapter 28 Test: The Roman Empire

A. Matching. Match each god or goddess with the correct description.

_____ 1. Jupiter   a. the Roman god of the sea

_____ 2. Mars   b. the king of the Roman gods

_____ 3. Neptune   c. the daughter of the goddess of the harvest

_____ 4. Ceres   d. the king of the underworld

_____ 5. Proserpine   e. the goddess of the harvest

_____ 6. Pluto   f. the Roman god of war

B. Multiple Choice. Circle the letter of the best choice.

7. The Romans took the _____ gods as their own but gave them Roman names.

   a. Greek

   b. Babylonian

   c. Egyptian

   d. Assyrian

8. Which of the following did the Romans not build?

   a. roads

   b. apartment buildings

   c. castles

   d. baths

9. How did the Romans travel from one end of the Italian peninsula to the other?

   a. They built aqueducts.

   b. They built roads.

   c. They used ships.

   d. They did not travel much.

10. The Appian Way was a famous Roman _____.

       a. bath

       b. apartment building

       c. aqueduct

       d. road

11. The Romans built _____ to bring fresh water into the cities.

       a. baths

       b. gladiators

       c. aqueducts

       d. roads

12. _____ were men trained to fight with each other and with wild animals.

       a. gladiators

       b. consuls

       c. patricians

       d. aqueducts

C. True or False. Write the word "true" or "false."

_____ 13. According to the Romans, winter comes because Ceres has to spend six months of every year in the underworld.

_____ 14. The Romans were the first ancient people to use concrete.

_____ 15. The Roman roads were much better than most roads of the ancient world.

_____ 16. All Roman apartment buildings were well built and luxurious.

_____ 17. Today, many things built by the Romans can still be found.

_____ 18. The Romans were bloodthirsty people; they liked to see men hurt.

Name _____   Date _____

Chapter 29 Test: Rome's War with Carthage

A. Fill in the blanks.

1. Rome and Carthage fought for many years in the _____.

2. At first, Carthage had the advantage because they had a _____, soldiers who knew how to sail ships.

3. _____ was a famous general from Carthage.

4. _____ was the man who finally defeated him.

B. Multiple Choice. Circle the letter of the best choice.

5. Why did Rome and Carthage fight for so many years?

   a. The both wanted to control trade around the Mediterranean Sea.

   b. Rome wanted to take over all of the Carthaginian land.

   c. Carthage wanted to take over all of the Roman land.

   d. They both wanted to rule India.

6. How did the Romans learn how to build ships like the Carthaginians?

   a. They captured some Carthaginian soldiers.

   b. The Romans sent spies to Carthage.

   c. A Carthaginian sailor betrayed his country and moved to Rome.

   d. They took apart a Carthaginian ship that wrecked on the coast of Italy.

7. A Roman general named Claudius Pulcher took sacred _____ on his ship to bring him good fortune in battle.

   a. elephants

   b. cows

   c. chickens

   d. peacocks

8. What unusual thing did the Carthaginians use to attack the Romans?

    a. elephants

    b. cannons

    c. ships

9. How did the Carthaginians sneak into Italy?

    a. They came over the mountains.

    b. They came at night.

    c. They sailed on ships.

    d. They came through Greece.

10. How did the Roman general get the Carthaginians to leave Italy?

    a. He pretended to surrender.

    b. He drove them out with his strong army.

    c. He attacked the city of Carthage.

    d. He surrounded their camp and starved them.

11. Who finally won these wars?

    a. Carthage

    b. Rome

    c. Gaul

    d. Greece

C. True or False. Write the word "true" or "false."

_____ 12. After the Romans took over all of Italy, they were content and peaceful.

_____ 13. The wars between Rome and Carthage took place mainly on land.

_____ 14. The Romans made many sacrifices to their gods asking for help in defeating Carthage.

_____ 15. When the great general of Carthage heard that the war was over, he killed himself by drinking poison.

The Story of the World

Chapter 30 Test: The Aryans of India

A. Fill in the blanks.

1. The Aryans were a group of people who came to India from _____.

2. The Aryans settled near two rivers, the Indus River and the _____ River.

3. The religion of these people was called _____.

4. In this religion, people belong to one of four groups called a _____.

B. Multiple Choice. Circle the letter of the best choice.

5. What kinds of crops did the Indian farmers raise?

    a. wheat and rice

    b. melons and wheat

    c. corn and beans

    d. cotton and rice

6. Every year the sacred river in India would _____.

    a. dry up

    b. overflow

    c. change direction

    d. grow longer

7. Who did the people of ancient India believe had given them their river?

    a. Siddhartha

    b. Rig Veda

    c. Ganga

    d. Shiva

8. Which group of people was the most important?

    a. farmers and traders

    b. noble warriors

    c. brahmin or priests

    d. untouchables

9. How did people know which group they belonged to?

    a. They were born into it.

    b. They married into it.

    c. They were assigned a group at school.

    d. They were assigned a group by the king.

10. What were the people called who didn't belong to any group?

    a. farmers and traders

    b. noble warriors

    c. brahmin or priests

    d. untouchables

11. Why did Siddhartha leave his palace?

    a. He was bored.

    b. He wanted to see what was outside the palace walls.

    c. He thought that a god was calling him to go.

    d. He wanted to help people.

12. Siddhartha became known as _____.

    a. Shiva

    b. Ganga

    c. Buddha

    d. Purusha

C. True or False. Write the word "true" or "false."

_____ 13. The people of ancient India raised horses and cows.

_____ 14. The job of the Untouchables was to protect the priests from enemies and to rule India.

_____ 15. In India, you could only marry someone who belonged to the same group as you.

_____ 16. Siddhartha taught that people could find happiness by leading a good life.

_____ 17. Today, no one follows the teachings of Siddhartha.

Name _____   Date _____

Chapter 31 Test: The Mauryan Empire of India

A. Fill in the blanks.

1. Cities in the ancient world were stronger if they were _____ together with other cities.

2. _____ was a famous ruler of the Mauryan Empire.

3. He followed the religious teachings of _____.

4. Some of the best-known writings from the Mahayana Tripitaka are called the _____.

B. Multiple Choice. Circle the letter of the best choice.

5. Why did the Indian kings want to unite the many different cities?

   a. They wanted India to be a strong, unified country.

   b. They wanted to be able to attack other countries.

   c. They needed to help each other with farming.

   d. They wanted to be like their neighbors.

6. Why did Asoka not want to fight with an army?

   a. He did not have enough money to pay his soldiers.

   b. He did not think he could trust an army.

   c. He wanted to defeat everyone by himself.

   d. He saw the suffering that his soldiers had caused.

7. Asoka made laws against _____.

   a. eating meat

   b. having hospitals

   c. being cruel to animals

   d. dishonesty

8. A vegetarian is someone who _____.

    a. does not allow violence

    b. doesn't eat meat

    c. takes care of animals

9. Asoka became famous for _____.

    a. his just, merciful rule

    b. the thousands of people he killed

    c. the trees he planted

    d. his strict, harsh commands

10. According to legend, the Jakata Tales were told by _____ to show people how to live.

    a. Asoka

    b. Sakka

    c. Buddha

    d. Jackal

11. In the story we read from the Jakata Tales, who was rewarded for his generosity?

    a. the monkey

    b. the hare

    c. the otter

    d. the jackal

12. Why were the other animals not rewarded?

    a. They would not share any food.

    b. They stole their food.

    c. They did not find any food.

    d. They only ate grass.

C. True or False. Write the word "true" or "false."

_____ 13. It was very unusual for ancient cities to be united together.

_____ 14. Asoka planted trees along the road so that travelers could walk in the shade.

_____ 15. Asoka built hospitals for sick people and sick animals.

_____ 16. King Asoka gave up eating meat because of the teachings of Sakka.

Name _____ Date _____

Chapter 32 Test: China: Writing and the Qin

A. Fill in the blanks.

1. Ancient China was divided into _____ separate kingdoms with their own rulers and armies.

2. The ruler of each kingdom was called the _____.

3. These kingdoms were constantly fighting, so this time period is called "The Period of the

   _____."

4. The ruler of the kingdom of _____ conquered all of the other kingdoms and became the first emperor of all China.

B. Multiple Choice. Circle the letter of the best choice.

5. The first Chinese writing used pictures that looked almost exactly like the words they represented, but later Chinese writing began to change into writing that looked less like the words they stood for. This kind of writing is called _____.

   a. pictograms

   b. calligraphy

   c. hieroglyphics

   d. cuneiform

6. In this form of writing, each word is called a _____.

   a. pictogram

   b. cuneiform

   c. calligraph

   d. character

7. Writers in ancient China first used special sharp paintbrushes made out of _____.

   a. animal hair

   b. grasses & reeds

   c. copper fibers

   d. clay that had been hardened

8. The Chinese were the first people to use _____ with ink and blocks of wood.

    a. clay tablets

    b. cuneiform

    c. printing

    d. papyrus

9. What did Qin Zheng do to keep control of his new kingdom?

    a. He made all of the former rulers move to his capital city so he could keep an eye on them.

    b. He killed anyone who tried to rebel against him

    c. He burned thousands of books.

    d. All of the above

10. What did the people think about Qin Zheng?

    a. They loved him.

    b. They despised him for his cruelty.

    c. They thought he was fair and just.

    d. They worshipped him as a god.

11. Why did Qin Zheng build the Great Wall of China?

    a. He didn't want any of his people to escape.

    b. He wanted to keep the Mongols out of China.

    c. He was worried about the Mauryan Empire in India.

    d. He wanted to be remembered forever.

12. What is the Great Wall of China made of?

    a. carved blocks of stone

    b. sun-baked clay

    c. rocks from the river beds

    d. stone and packed dirt

C. True or False. Write the word "true" or "false."

_____ 13. Qin Zheng changed his name to Shi Huangdi meaning "Emperor of the Sun."

_____ 14. It took one hundred years to build the Great Wall of China.

_____ 15. The Great Wall of China is almost as long as the United States is wide.

_____ 16. Archaeologists found thousands of life-sized clay horses and soldiers around Qin Zheng's tomb.

The Story of the World

Chapter 33 Test: Confucius

A. Multiple Choice. Circle the letter of the best choice.

1. Confucius lived around the same time as _____.

    a. Alexander the Great

    b. Buddha

    c. Abraham

    d. Qin Zheng

2. Like Buddha, Confucius taught that people could learn to be _____ even if they were poor.

    a. wealthy

    b. smart

    c. happy

    d. sad

3. Confucius hated _____, which was happening all around him.

    a. war

    b. wealth

    c. peace

    d. wastefulness

4. He taught that people should _____ authority.

    a. respect

    b. rebel against

    c. ignore

    d. disobey

5. He also taught that people in authority should be _____ to those who are beneath them.

    a. kind

    b. cruel

    c. just

    d. hateful

6. The sayings of Confucius were collected together into a book called _____.

      a. *The Sayings of Confucius*

      b. *The Writings of Confucius*

      c. *The Wisdom of Confucius*

      d. *The Analects of Confucius*

C. True or False. Write the word "true" if the statement is one of the saying of Confucius or "false" if it is not.

_____ 7. Do not do unto others, what you would not want others to do to you.

_____ 8. If you make a mistake and correct it, this is a bigger mistake.

_____ 9. It is the wiser person who takes rather than gives.

_____ 10. He who aims to be a man of complete virtue does not seek to gratify his appetite in his food.

The Story of the World

Chapter 34 Test: The Rise of Julius Caesar

A. Fill in the blanks.

1. Julius Caesar was born in _____.

2. His family claimed to be descended from _____, the founder of Rome.

3. His uncle was a _____, one of Rome's two rulers.

4. At one time, Caesar's job was governing the Roman province of _____.

B. Multiple Choice. Circle the letter of the best choice.

5. What is rhetoric?

   a. public speaking

   b. reading

   c. writing

   d. mathematics

6. What happened when Caesar sailed out to an island in the Mediterranean Sea to take more rhetoric lessons?

   a. He was shipwrecked.

   b. His ship became lost.

   c. He became ill and almost died.

   d. He was captured by pirates.

7. What event caused everyone in Rome to know who Caesar was?

   a. He won a rhetoric competition.

   b. He won a great victory in Gaul.

   c. He captured pirates and had them executed.

   d. He was elected to the Senate.

8. Why could Caesar not become consul when he wanted to?

   a. He was not old enough.

   b. He could not get elected.

   c. He was out of the country.

   d. There were already two consuls.

9. Caesar wept when he read the story of Alexander the Great because _____.

      a. Caesar had not yet done anything to make himself famous

      b. he was sad that Alexander died so young

      c. he wanted a great horse like Bucephalus

      d. he had never been to Greece and really wanted to go

10. Caesar was not popular with _____.

      a. the people

      b. his soldiers

      c. the rich, powerful men of Rome

      d. his family

11. The Senate worried that Caesar wanted to be _____.

      a. the most powerful Senator

      b. the king of Rome

      c. the ruler of Egypt

      d. the ruler of Spain

12. The Senators wished that Caesar were more like _____.

      a. Alexander the Great

      b. Cincinnatus

      c. Romulus

      d. Scipio

C. True or False. Write the word "true" or "false."

_____ 13. Caesar's father once said that his son would "become one of the most famous men in Rome!"

_____ 14. Caesar became popular by throwing large parties for the people he needed to vote for him.

_____ 15. Caesar was excited about his job of governing one of Rome's colonies.

_____ 16. When Caesar became consul, the consuls were known as the triumvirate because there were three of them.

_____ 17. Caesar always listened to the Senators and did what they said.

_____ 18. Cincinnatus was a legendary Roman who represented the ideal ruler.

The Story of the World

Chapter 35 Test: Caesar the Hero

A. Fill in the blanks.

1. Julius Caesar wanted to conquer a country called _____.

2. The people who lived in this country were the _____

3. The _____ convinced Pompey to turn against Caesar.

4. Caesar went to _____ to look for Pompey.

5. While he was there, Caesar fell in love with _____.

B. Multiple Choice. Circle the letter of the best choice.

6. Caesar's soldiers were loyal to him because _____.

   a. he treated them so well

   b. he paid them well

   c. he made sure they had plenty to eat

   d. All of the above.

7. Why was it hard to convince Pompey to turn against Caesar?

   a. Pompey was jealous of Caesar.

   b. Pompey had married Caesar's daughter.

   c. Pompey knew that Caesar was more popular with the people than he was.

   d. Pompey thought that Caesar was a great hero.

8. What message did Pompey send to Caesar?

   a. Caesar would be arrested when he returned to Rome.

   b. Pompey would give up his job as consul.

   c. Caesar would be made king when he returned to Rome.

   d. Caesar would be killed when he returned to Rome.

9. Caesar had to cross the _____ River to return to Rome.

    a. Rubicon

    b. Tiber

    c. Euphrates

    d. Ganges

10. Why was it hard for Pompey to find soldiers to fight for him?

    a. No one liked Pompey.

    b. Pompey did not have enough money to pay them.

    c. All of the men who were the right age already belonged to Caesar's army.

    d. No one wanted to fight against Caesar's army.

11. What did the two pharaohs of Egypt do to try to make friends with Caesar?

    a. They gave Caesar many gifts of gold and jewels.

    b. They sent Pompey to Caesar as a prisoner.

    c. They sent Pompey's head to Caesar in a bag.

    d. They gave Caesar part of Egypt.

12. What happened to Caesar on March 15, 44 BC?

    a. He was crowned as king.

    b. He was killed in the Senate.

    c. He became the new pharaoh of Egypt.

    d. He was named dictator for life.

C. True or False. Write the word "true" or "false."

_____ 13. When Caesar sent back reports to the Roman people about the wars he was fighting, he was always honest about the times when he was defeated.

_____ 14. "Veni, vidi, vici" means "I came, I saw, I conquered" in Latin.

_____ 15. Caesar was made king when he returned from Egypt.

_____ 16. Caesar wanted his adopted son, Octavian, to inherit his power.

_____ 17. Caesar's wife begged him not to go to the Senate on March 15.

_____ 18. Many of Caesar's friends turned against him, but Brutus remained loyal.

Name _____ Date _____

Chapter 36 Test: The First Roman Prince

A. Fill in the blanks.

1. Octavian's uncle and adopted father was _____.

2. The month of _____ was named after Octavian.

3. The month of _____ was named after Julius Caesar.

4. Octavian became Rome's first _____.

B. Multiple Choice. Circle the letter of the best choice.

5. When Julius Caesar died, Octavian _____.

   a. threw a huge party that lasted for ten days

   b. hid in Egypt

   c. became the new king

   d. refused to see anyone

6. Octavian went to the Senate and demanded that _____.

   a. Caesar be honored with a special statue

   b. Caesar's murderers be put to death

   c. he be made the new emperor

   d. he be made a consul

7. The Senate did not want Octavian to become a leader of Rome because _____.

   a. he was too old

   b. the people did not like him

   c. he was too much like Caesar

   d. he did not have enough money

8. How was Octavian like Julius Caesar?

   a. He made many enemies in the Roman Senate.

   b. He demanded that the Senate make him king.

   c. He fell in love with Cleopatra.

   d. He made the Roman Empire bigger and richer.

9. The Senate gave Octavian the title of _____.

     a. First Citizen

     b. dictator for life

     c. emperor

     d. consul for life

10. The Senate also changed Octavian's name to _____.

     a. Julius Caesar

     b. Princeps Caesar

     c. Augustus Caesar

     d. Cincinnatus Caesar

C. True or False. Write the word "true" or "false."

_____ 11. After Julius Caesar died, Rome was finally at peace.

_____ 12. Octavian was only nineteen when Caesar died.

_____ 13. Octavian gave presents and money to every rich family in Rome.

_____ 14. Octavian's new name meant "blessed" and "majestic."

_____ 15. The English word "prince" comes from the Latin word "princeps."

The Story of the World

Chapter 37 Test: The Beginning of Christianity

A. Fill in the blanks.

1. The time of peace and safety in the Roman Empire was called the _____.

2. We can read about Jesus in the four books of the Bible called the _____.

3. According to the Bible, Jesus was born in _____.

4. Many people celebrate the birth of Jesus on _____.

5. The people who followed Jesus became known as _____.

B. Multiple Choice. Circle the letter of the best choice.

6. Jesus was born in an area called Judea which was once known as _____.

    a. Phoenicia

    b. Canaan

    c. Syria

    d. Jerusalem

7. _____ was the mother of Jesus.

    a. Anna

    b. Elizabeth

    c. Mary

    d. Sarah

8. Why did Jesus' parents have to take a trip just before he was born?

    a. They wanted to be with their families when the baby was born.

    b. Augustus Caesar ordered that everyone in the Roman Empire go back to the place were their ancestors were from to be counted.

    c. They were looking for new jobs.

    d. The king of Judea ordered everyone to move to a new place to be counted.

9. Angels announced the birth of Jesus to a group of _____.

    a. shepherds

    b. kings

    c. servants

    d. women

10. When Jesus grew up, his most famous teaching was given _____.

    a. to the chief priests

    b. in the temple

    c. to Augustus Caesar

    d. on the side of a mountain

11. The Gospel of Luke says that after Jesus died, he was put into a tomb, and after three days _____.

    a. he came back to life

    b. his followers began mourning for him

    c. he went to heaven

    d. he appeared to Caesar Augustus

12. The years after Jesus' birth are called _____.

    a. BC

    b. BCE

    c. AD

    d. AC

C. True or False. Write the word "true" or "false."

_____ 13. During the time when Jesus was born, it was dangerous to travel on the Mediterranean Sea.

_____ 14. Jesus' mother worshipped the God of Abraham.

_____ 15. The Sermon on the Mount contains many of Jesus' teachings.

_____ 16. Jesus was not very popular with the people of Judea.

_____ 17. The Romans were worried that Jesus might decide he wanted to become the king of the Jews.

_____ 18. "Anno Domini" means "The Year of Our Lord" in Latin.

Name _____ Date _____

Chapter 38 Test: The End of the Ancient Jewish Nation

A. Fill in the blanks.

1. _____ was the father of the Jewish nation.

2. Jacob had _____ sons who became the tribes of Israel.

3. The Israelites lived in _____ until the Assyrians captured them.

4. _____ was the good king of Persia and Babylon who allowed the Jews to move back to their own land.

5. Around the time of Jesus' life, the Jews were ruled by the _____.

B. Multiple Choice. Circle the letter of the best choice.

6. When Joseph lived in Egypt, the Israelites joined him there because _____.

    a. they missed Joseph so much

    b. they thought they could become rich in Egypt

    c. a famine had destroyed all their crops

    d. they wanted to worship the Egyptian gods

7. Why didn't the Jews like the Romans?

    a. The Romans forced them to pay high taxes.

    b. The Romans would not let them stay in their own country.

    c. The Romans wouldn't let them worship God.

    d. The Romans made them their slaves.

8. The Jews worshipped God in the Temple in the city of _____.

    a. Rome

    b. Jerusalem

    c. Bethlehem

    d. Nazareth

9. What did the Jews do when they rebelled against Rome?

    a. They set fire to the house of the Roman ruler of Judea.

    b. Armed groups of Jewish men attacked Roman soldiers.

    c. They killed the emperor.

    d. a and b

10. What did the Romans do when the Jews rebelled?

    a. They killed all of the Jews.

    b. They ignored the Jews and let them have their country.

    c. They burned down the Temple.

    d. c and d

11. What happened to all of the gold and silver decorations inside the Temple?

    a. The Jews hid them from the Romans.

    b. They melted into the cracks between the stones of the Temple's foundations.

    c. The Jews sold them to help pay for their fight against the Romans.

    d. The Jews gave them to the Romans.

12. What happened to the Jews?

    a. They were scattered throughout all the countries of the ancient world.

    b. They remained in Canaan, but were never again a strong nation.

    c. They conquered the Romans.

    d. They were all killed.

C. True or False. Write the word "true" or "false."

_____ 13. Other countries ruled the Jews for many years.

_____ 14. The Romans never worried about countries rebelling against them.

_____ 15. The Temple was destroyed, all the way down to its foundation.

_____ 16. The Jews have never returned to the land of Canaan.

The Story of the World

Chapter 39 Test: Rome and the Christians

A. Fill in the blanks.

1. Nero, the worst Roman emperor of all, loved _____ even though he was terrible at it.

2. When Rome burned, Nero blamed the _____.

3. The Christians held meetings in underground passages called _____.

4. Constantine built a new capital city for the Roman Empire called _____.

B. Multiple Choice. Circle the letter of the best choice.

5. Why were people so afraid of Nero?

    a. Nero was so similar to Augustus Caesar.

    b. Nero tried to put spells on people.

    c. Nero had everyone who disagreed with him murdered.

    d. Nero stole money from a lot of people.

6. When the city of Rome burned, Nero was _____.

    a. watching from his palace

    b. visiting Egypt

    c. in another city at a meeting

    d. in the country giving a huge party

7. What did Nero do when he heard about the fire?

    a. He gave money to all of the poor families.

    b. He rebuilt all of the buildings that had been burned down.

    c. He stayed where he was for several more days.

    d. He built a new capital city.

8. The Roman emperors did not like the Christians because the Christians _____.

    a. would not worship the emperor

    b. were becoming wealthier than the Romans

    c. disobeyed all of the Roman laws

    d. were encouraging the Roman people to rebel

9. The Christians used a _____ as a secret symbol to identify other Christians.

    a. fish

    b. cross

    c. Greek word for Jesus

    d. dove

10. Constantine ended the persecution of the Christians because _____.

    a. he was a Christian too

    b. he didn't think it was right to put people in jail because of who they worshipped

    c. he wanted the Christians to think he was a good emperor

    d. the Christians paid him a lot of money

11. What did Constantine see in the sky before an important battle?

    a. a fish made out of clouds

    b. a picture of Jesus

    c. a cross of light

    d. the army of God

12. What happened to Constantine after the battle?

    a. He started persecuting the Christians again.

    b. He became a Christian.

    c. He returned to Rome.

    d. He took a trip to Jerusalem

C. True or False. Write the word "true" or "false."

_____ 13. The Roman army often refused to obey the emperors because they were such bad generals.

_____ 14. One emperor made his horse a consul and told everyone to obey the horse.

_____ 15. The Roman people were grateful to Nero for helping them after the burning of Rome.

_____ 16. The Romans worshipped the emperor as one of their gods.

_____ 17. Many Christians were forced to fight in gladiator shows or killed by wild animals during Nero's reign.

_____ 18. Constantine's army was defeated at the Battle of the Milvian Bridge.

The Story of the World

Chapter 40 Test: Rome Begins to Weaken

A. Fill in the blanks.

1. Boadicea was the leader of a tribe of _____ in the Roman province of Britain.

2. The Romans were embarrassed to be beaten by Boadicea because Boadicea was
   a _____.

3. _____ was the emperor who decided to divide the empire into two parts.

4. He ruled the _____ half and chose someone else to rule the other half.

B. Multiple Choice. Circle the letter of the best choice.

5. The Roman Empire began to weaken because _____.

    a. there were many bad emperors

    b. some of the countries that Rome had conquered began to rebel

    c. the empire was getting so large

    d. all of the above

6. Why did the Romans finally win against Boadicea?

    a. They had more men in their army.

    b. They had better weapons.

    c. They had better maps of the area.

    d. They stayed together in battle and obeyed their general.

7. Why did the size of the Roman Empire cause problems?

    a. The emperor could not visit all of the different cities to meet the people.

    b. There were no good roads to travel from one end of the empire to another.

    c. The borders were too long for one army to protect.

    d. There was not enough food for such a large empire.

8. When the empire was split, who was chosen to rule the other half of the empire?

    a. Boadicea

    b. Diocletian

    c. Constantine

    d. Maximian

9. _____ was the capital of the Western Roman Empire.

    a. Rome

    b. Gaul

    c. Constantinople

    d. Londinium

10. _____ was the capital of the Eastern Roman Empire.

    a. Rome

    b. Gaul

    c. Constantinople

    d. Londinium

11. Why did the Romans call the people who invaded them "barbarians"?

    a. They thought they were crude and uncivilized.

    b. They could not understand their language.

    c. They were not Christians.

    d. Their weapons had sharp points called barbs on them.

C. True or False. Write the word "true" or "false."

_____ 12. Julius Caesar and Augustus Caesar were two of Rome's strongest rulers.

_____ 13. The Roman settlement of Londinium became the city of London.

_____ 14. The Romans conquered all of the British Isles, but they did not stay in control for long.

_____ 15. Invaders attacked the Roman Empire in Britain, Gaul, Spain and Italy itself.

_____ 16. If you go to Italy today, you will not see any remains of the Roman Empire.

The Story of the World

Chapter 41 Test: The Attacking Barbarians

A. Fill in the blanks.

1. The Huns were a group of barbarians from Central Asia who attacked Rome on strong, fast _____.

2. _____ was a brave Roman fighter whose father was a barbarian.

3. The _____ were a group of barbarians who destroyed the city of Rome.

B. Multiple Choice. Circle the letter of the best choice.

4. The leader of the Huns was _____.

   a. Honoria

   b. Attila

   c. Alaric

   d. Stilicho

5. The Roman emperor's sister sent a letter to the leader of the Huns offering to _____.

   a. surrender to him

   b. give him thousands of pounds of gold

   c. introduce him to her brother

   d. marry him

6. Why did the Huns leave Italy after a successful invasion?

   a. The emperor paid them a large amount of money.

   b. The emperor gave their leader his sister in marriage.

   c. The Roman army drove them back out.

   d. The did not like living in Rome.

7. What happened to the Huns' leader before he could marry the emperor's sister?

   a. A Roman soldier killed him.

   b. His own men killed him.

   c. He died of a nosebleed.

   d. Another group of barbarians captured him.

8. How did Stilicho get the Visigoths to leave Rome?

    a. He gave them four thousand pounds of gold.

    b. He defeated them after many battles.

    c. He married the daughter of their leader.

    d. He killed their leader.

9. When the emperor heard that the Visigoths were again planning to invade Rome, he _____.

    a. killed himself

    b. gathered together a small army to defend the city

    c. fled to a small city in the middle of a swamp

    d. sent them a letter begging them to leave.

10. Why didn't the Eastern Roman Empire send help?

    a. They did not like the Western Roman Empire.

    b. The emperor was afraid that the barbarians would attack his own city.

    c. They had become allies with the Visigoths.

    d. They did send help, but it arrived too late.

11. When the Visigoths invaded the city of Rome, they _____.

    a. ripped down golden statues and stole coins and jewelry

    b. took the people of Rome as hostages

    c. destroyed Rome's churches

    d. did not harm anything in the city

C. True or False. Write the word "true" or "false."

_____ 12. The Huns taught their babies to ride horseback even before they could walk.

_____ 13. The Huns built a huge monument over the grave of their great leader.

_____ 14. Some barbarians grew to like the Roman way of life and sometimes switched sides.

_____ 15. Many Romans felt bad after they executed Stilicho.

_____ 16. When the Eastern Roman Empire heard that Rome had been invaded, they rejoiced.

Name _____ Date

The Story of the World

Chapter 42 Test: The End of Rome

A. Fill in the blanks.

1. After the Roman Empire divided, the Eastern Roman Empire became known as the
_____ Empire.

2. _____ was the last Roman emperor.

3. He was only _____ years old when he was named emperor.

B. Multiple Choice. Circle the letter of the best choice.

4. An invader named _____ decided to drive the Roman Emperor out of hiding.

    a. Alaric

    b. Attila

    c. Orestes

    d. Stilicho

5. When the emperor heard that he was coming he _____.

    a. ran away

    b. surrendered to him

    c. gathered an army for one last fight

    d. sent him thousands of pounds of gold

6. The Romans called their last emperor "Momyllus" which means _____.

    a. little ruler

    b. great ruler

    c. last

    d. little disgrace

7. What happened to the land that once belonged to Rome?

    a. It became part of the Eastern Roman empire.

    b. It was given to the Huns.

    c. It was divided among the various barbarian kings.

    d. It all became the country of France.

C. True or False. Write the word "true" or "false."

_____ 8. The Romans loved their last emperor.

_____ 9. When the people of the Eastern Roman Empire heard that the Western Roman Empire was gone, they mourned.

_____ 10. The Romans gave us many words and inventions that we use today.

D. Match each English word with the Latin word it comes from (one word will not be used).

_____ 11. refrigerator   a. scriptum

_____ 12. family   b. liber

_____ 13. library   c. floris

_____ 14. navy   d. navis

_____ 15. flower   e. familia

                           f. frigidarium

E. Name three things other than words that we get from the Romans.

16. _____

17. _____

18. _____

The Story of the World,
Volume 1: Ancient Times

ANSWER KEY

Chapter 1 Test

1. nomad
2. tents
3. caves
4. the Fertile Crescent
5. canals
6. b
7. c
8. d
9. a
10. c
11. b
12. b
13. true
14. false
15. true
16. false
17. false
18. true

Chapter 2 Test

1. Africa
2. flood
3. Lower Egyptians
4. Upper Egyptians
5. pharaoh
6. a
7. c
8. b
9. c
10. d
11. a
12. b
13. true
14. true
15. false
16. true
17. false
18. true

Chapter 3 Test

1. Egyptians
2. hieroglyphics
3. Sumer
4. cuneiforms
5. a
6. c
7. b
8. d
9. a
10. c
11. false
12. false
13. true
14. true
15. true

Chapter 4 Test

1. mummies
2. priests
3. heart
4. three
5. pyramids
6. b
7. a
8. d
9. b
10. a
11. b
12. true
13. true
14. true
15. false
16. false

Chapter 5 Test

1. Mesopotamia
2. Sumerians
3. city-states
4. Sargon
5. Kish
6. d
7. b
8. a
9. c
10. c
11. true
12. true
13. false
14. false
15. true

Chapter 6 Test

1. Ur
2. Genesis
3. Canaan
4. twelve
5. Egypt
6. a
7. c
8. d
9. a
10. b
11. d
12. c
13. true
14. false
15. true
16. true
17. false
18. false

Chapter 7 Test

1. Babylonia
2. The Code of Hammurabi
3. one year
4. twelve
5. a
6. d
7. c
8. d
9. a
10. b
11. true
12. false
13. true
14. true
15. false

Chapter 8 Test

1. northern
2. Assyrian
3. Gilgamesh
4. snake
5. b
6. b
7. a
8. d
9. c
10. a
11. true
12. true
13. false
14. true
15. false

Chapter 9 Test

1. trading
2. rivers
3. Indus River
4. citadels
5. c
6. c
7. a
8. b
9. d
10. a
11. false
12. true
13. true
14. false
15. true

Chapter 10 Test

1. Yellow
2. rice
3. silk
4. dynasty
5. pictograms
6. b
7. c
8. b
9. a
10. d
11. d
12. a
13. true
14. true
15. true
16. false
17. false
18. true

Chapter 11 Test

1. Sahara Desert
2. oasis
3. water
4. Anansi the Spider
5. a
6. d
7. a
8. b
9. b
10. d
11. true
12. true
13. true
14. false
15. true

Chapter 12 Test

1. Nubia
2. Kush
3. dynasty
4. Canaan
5. c
6. a
7. d
8. a
9. b
10. b
11. c
12. false
13. true
14. false
15. false
16. true

Chapter 13 Test

1. b
2. d
3. a
4. c
5. true
6. false
7. false
8. false
9. true
10. d
11. a
12. a
13. c
14. b
15. b
16. d
17. c

Chapter 14 Test

1. Abraham
2. slaves
3. Moses
4. Red Sea
5. Exodus
6. a
7. d
8. c
9. c
10. a
11. b
12. d
13. true
14. false
15. false
16. false
17. true
18. true

Chapter 15 Test

1. Canaan
2. Mediterranean Sea
3. Carthage
4. Tyre
5. d
6. b
7. c
8. c
9. a
10. c
11. false
12. true
13. true
14. false
15. true

Chapter 16 Test

1. baskets
2. cruel
3. Nineveh
4. librarian
5. c
6. b
7. a
8. a
9. d
10. c
11. true
12. true
13. false
14. true
15. false

Chapter 17 Test

1. animal
2. Daniel
3. Persia
4. Hanging Gardens
5. a
6. c
7. b
8. a
9. d
10. b
11. c
12. false
13. true
14. false
15. false
16. true

Chapter 18 Test

1. Minoans
2. Mediterranean
3. bulls
4. navy
5. Minotaur
6. b
7. c
8. b
9. a
10. d
11. c
12. a
13. c
14. false
15. true
16. true
17. false
18. true

Chapter 19 Test

1. c
2. b
3. a
4. d
5. a
6. a
7. c
8. b
9. c
10. d
11. b
12. a
13. true
14. true
15. false
16. false

Chapter 20 Test

1. d
2. c
3. a
4. b
5. c
6. a
7. a
8. b
9. d
10. b
11. a
12. c
13. true
14. true
15. false
16. true
17. false
18. false

Chapter 21 Test

1. Medes
2. shepherds
3. Cyrus
4. Greece
5. a
6. d
7. c
8. d
9. a
10. c
11. b
12. b
13. true
14. false
15. true
16. true
17. false
18. true

Chapter 22 Test

1. Athens
2. Sparta
3. forum
4. democracy
5. b
6. c
7. a
8. d
9. a
10. b
11. b
12. d
13. d
14. false
15. false
16. true
17. true
18. false

Chapter 23 Test

1. b
2. f
3. e
4. h
5. d
6. c
7. a
8. g
9. c
10. a
11. d
12. d
13. h
14. c
15. a
16. true
17. false
18. true

Chapter 24 Test

1. Athens   2. Persia   3. Parthenon   4. Sparta   5. a
6. d   7. c   8. b   9. a   10. c
11. b   12. b   13. true   14. false   15. false
16. true   17. true   18. false

Chapter 25 Test

1. Macedonia   2. Persian   3. lighthouse   4. Alexandria   5. c
6. c   7. a   8. d   9. b   10. d
11. c   12. false   13. true   14. true   15. true
16. false

Chapter 26 Test

1. Atlantic   2. Central America   3. mountains   4. written records   5. a
6. d   7. c   8. d   9. c   10. c
11. b   12. b   13. false   14. true   15. false
16. true

Chapter 27 Test

1. seven   2. Italy   3. Etruscans   4. togas   5. b
6. a   7. c   8. d   9. d   10. a
11. b   12. d   13. true   14. false   15. true
16. false

Chapter 28 Test

1. b   2. f   3. a   4. e   5. c
6. d   7. a   8. c   9. b   10. d
11. c   12. a   13. false   14. true   15. true
16. false   17. true   18. true

Chapter 29 Test

1. Punic Wars   2. navy   3. Hannibal   4. Scipio   5. a
6. d   7. c   8. a   9. a   10. c
11. b   12. false   13. false   14. true   15. true

Chapter 30 Test

1. Asia   2. Ganges   3. Hinduism   4. caste   5. a
6. b   7. d   8. c   9. a   10. d
11. b   12. c   13. true   14. false   15. true
16. true   17. false

Chapter 31 Test

1. united   2. Asoka   3. Buddha   4. Jakata Tales   5. a
6. d   7. c   8. b   9. a   10. c
11. b   12. b   13. false   14. true   15. true
16. false

Chapter 32 Test

1. six
2. warlord
3. Warring States
4. Qin
5. b
6. d
7. a
8. c
9. d
10. b
11. b
12. d
13. false
14. false
15. true
16. true

Chapter 33 Test

1. b
2. c
3. a
4. a
5. a
6. d
7. true
8. false
9. false
10. true

Chapter 34 Test

1. Rome
2. Romulus
3. consul
4. Spain
5. a
6. d
7. c
8. d
9. a
10. c
11. b
12. b
13. true
14. true
15. false
16. true
17. false
18. true

Chapter 35 Test

1. Britain
2. Celts
3. Senate
4. Egypt
5. Cleopatra
6. d
7. b
8. a
9. a
10. d
11. c
12. b
13. false
14. true
15. false
16. true
17. true
18. false

Chapter 36 Test

1. Julius Caesar
2. August
3. July
4. emperor
5. a
6. d
7. c
8. d
9. a
10. c
11. false
12. true
13. false
14. true
15. true

Chapter 37 Test

1. Pax Romana
2. Gospels
3. Bethlehem
4. Christmas
5. Christians
6. b
7. c
8. b
9. a
10. d
11. a
12. c
13. false
14. true
15. true
16. false
17. true
18. true

Chapter 38 Test

1. Abraham
2. twelve
3. Canaan
4. Cyrus
5. Romans
6. c
7. a
8. b
9. d
10. c
11. b
12. a
13. true
14. false
15. true
16. false

Chapter 39 Test

1. music
2. Christians
3. catacombs
4. Constantinople
5. c
6. d
7. c
8. a
9. a
10. b
11. c
12. b
13. true
14. true
15. false
16. true
17. true
18. false

Chapter 40 Test

1. Celts
2. woman
3. Diocletian
4. eastern
5. d
6. d
7. c
8. d
9. a
10. c
11. b
12. true
13. true
14. false
15. true
16. false

Chapter 41 Test

1. warhorses
2. Stilicho
3. Vandals
4. b
5. d
6. a
7. c
8. a
9. c
10. b
11. a
12. true
13. false
14. true
15. true
16. false

Chapter 42 Test

1. Byzantine
2. Romulus Augustus
3. six
4. c
5. a
6. d
7. c
8. false
9. true
10. true
11. f
12. e
13. b
14. d
15. c
16–18. answers will vary